BRITAIN IN O

FARNBOROUGH

JO GOSNEY

ALAN SUTTON PUBLISHING LIMITED

Alan Sutton Publishing Limited
Phoenix Mill · Far Thrupp · Stroud
Gloucestershire · GL5 2BU

First published 1995

Copyright © Jo Gosney, 1995

Cover photographs: (Front) Williamsons in
Victoria Road, *c.* 1909. (Back) Col. Cody's first
aeroplane, 1910.

British Library Cataloguing in Publication Data.
A catalogue record for this book is available from
the British Library.

ISBN 0–7509–0906–4

Typeset in 9/10 Sabon.
Typesetting and origination by
Alan Sutton Publishing Limited.
Printed in Great Britain by
Hartnolls, Bodmin, Cornwall.

The construction of the Clockhouse. In a prominent position on Farnborough Road, this building was completed in around 1895 and then occupied by Mrs Dever. The man in white overalls to the left, on the first level of scaffolding, is thought to be Mr Silvester, and another of the carpenters is Mr Gough.

Contents

	Introduction	5
1.	The Original Village	7
2.	The Arrival of the Army	15
3.	Empress Eugénie	23
4.	The Birth of Aviation	31
5.	Transport	43
6.	Religion	51
7.	Education	59
8.	People at Work	69
9.	Shopping Facilities	79
10.	Leisure Activities	93
11.	Streets and Buildings	107
	Acknowledgements	126

The fire brigade, *c.* 1905. This photograph was taken by Tudor Lawrence, a fireman, whose father-in-law, W.E. Fitch, was captain of the brigade. Jack Ward, a local farmer, is the driver; also on board are C.J. Morton, a local builder, and D. McLaurin. In the background is High Street, before the houses were erected, and beyond can be seen St Mark's School, opened in 1897.

Introduction

While researching for this book it has been my privilege to meet and talk with some of the oldest and most interesting residents of the town in my quest to discover what life was like in days gone by. Their pride in the town is reflected by the enthusiastic way in which they dug deep into their memories and family albums for material to show how Farnborough developed. Although a large number of photographs has been amassed here, there must still be many more tucked away in old drawers and cupboards. I hope this volume will encourage people to search them out and allow them to be reproduced; it would be very sad if such items of interest were to be mistakenly consigned to the bin or bonfire, to be lost forever. As they turn the pages, people may reflect nostalgically upon buildings long since demolished and pastimes now forgotten, but history is always in the making and we must continue to record these changes for future generations.

The first documented reference to Farnborough appears in the Domesday Book of 1086, when Ferneberga (meaning Fern Hill) is mentioned as being within the lands of the Bishop of Winchester. Ferneberga lay within the manor of Crondal, held by Odin of Windsore. It comprised farms and woodland and had one mill; the population consisted of one landowner, seven farmers, four cottagers and five serfs. This sleepy little village, once on the edge of Windsor Forest, was suddenly awoken in the 1850s by the arrival of the army in nearby Aldershot. Even the advent of the railway ten years earlier had not had such a dramatic effect upon the lives of the villagers. Murray's *First Handbook to Hampshire*, published in 1858, proclaimed: 'Farnborough – one of the gates of the Camp at Aldershott [*sic*]. The assemblage of Red Tunics, usually encountered at the station itself, and the half dozen taverns which have grouped themselves about it, sufficiently indicate that the camp is at no great distance.'

At that time photography was in its infancy and there were few cameras in private use. However, the army provided a ready market, encouraging a number of professional photographers to set up in business. The development of cameras and the increased prosperity in the town soon encouraged amateurs to record the events of the day. Thus we are the fortunate beneficiaries of this pictorial legacy, which illustrates the development of a small village. From a population of around five hundred in 1851 it has grown into a hi-tech town with a population of approximately 49,500.

The development of aviation also had an important impact upon Farnborough, and the quiet, rural community, graced by the presence of a few wealthy landowners, soon became a bustling town. Today Farnborough is renowned throughout the world for its biennial International Air Show. Recent demilitarization and rationalization in the aircraft industry have had their effect but the skills and expertise gained in aviation technology over the years have attracted many allied businesses to the town. This, along with Farnborough's proximity to the motorway network, has resulted in an ever increasing demand for housing. In 1932 the nearby village of Cove was incorporated into the Urban District of Farnborough. Then, as a consequence of local government reorganization in 1974, Farnborough was amalgamated with the adjacent Borough of Aldershot to form the present administrative Borough of Rushmoor.

All these rapid changes have caused the rise and decline of various parts of the town. Today in the north there are only a few cottages left to remind us of the original village. The administrative, commercial and residential aspects are now concentrated in the centre, with a brand new retail area to the far north on Farnborough Green (now called Farnborough Gate). In the area now known as North Camp, in south Farnborough, which for many years was the commercial hub of the town, there is still evidence of its former glory in some of the imposing buildings which remain.

Home Farm, c. 1902. This was one of the farms along Ship Lane on the Farnborough Hill estate. The buildings on the right have been demolished and the farm has now been built on, but the farmhouse itself remains as a private dwelling.

Section One

THE ORIGINAL

VILLAGE

A group of children gathered in Farnborough

Street, 1884.

Thomas Longman
builder of
Farnborough Hill 1863

This pen portrait by Miss Olive Chichester, granddaughter of Thomas Longman, shows a sketch of the house built by Mr Longman. The black swan and the ship are trademarks used by the Longman publishing firm and can still be seen on the building.

The wedding of Alice Longman in 1869. Thomas Longman's fourth daughter married Hugh Chichester (later Col. Chichester) on 22 September. The wedding guests, resplendent in their beautiful clothes are on the south lawn and to the right, a military band is providing music for the grand occasion. Clearly visible is much of the neo-gothic architecture of this ornate mansion, designed by Henry Edward Kendall and completed in 1863, when the Longmans took up residence. Many literary personalities of the day were entertained at Farnborough Hill, including Charles Kingsley who was vicar of Eversley and author of *The Water Babies*, James Froude and Henry Reeve. The Longman family were much loved by the villagers and did a great deal to improve their lives. The ladies often visited the poor and sick and Mr Longman gave some land for the first church school, built in 1868. Many parties were also given for all the local schoolchildren. After Mr Longman died in 1879 the mansion was sold to Empress Eugénie.

Street Farm, *c.* 1903. These listed buildings, dating from the seventeenth century, are some of the few ancient properties left relatively intact. Once the centre of village life in Farnborough, they have served as farmhouse, dairy, bacon curer's, shop and function rooms, and have now been converted into four cottages. Empress Cottages are to the right.

Windmill Hill before 1860. This was an earlier building on Farnborough Hill. It was built by James Ludovick Grant and sold to Mr Foreman. When Mrs Foreman died in 1836 it was then occupied by Lady Palmer and later bought by Thomas Longman in 1860. He demolished it and built Farnborough Hill.

Farnborough Street, 1884. All the local children have come out to see the photographer, who must have been quite a curiosity in this, the oldest, part of the village. Perhaps it is a Sunday or a holiday as they all appear to be wearing their best clothes. In the foreground, to the left, is Chandler the baker and beyond the gap is a row of four cottages, all of which have long since been demolished. Further on is Elm Tree Cottage, in front of which is the Old Pollard, an ancient elm tree with a huge girth and hollow inside, which had been at the centre of village activities for many years. In 1797 it was referred to in the churchwarden's accounts when the village seat was repaired. Later local blacksmith Mr Bartlett erected a 6 ft railing around it to prevent local tramps from sleeping in it, but sadly the tree was removed by the Council in 1917. In the distance is Street Farm. The tall gentleman in the centre of the photograph is Robert McLaurin, who was bailiff to Thomas Longman at Farnborough Hill and subsequently to Empress Eugénie. The small child in front of Mr McLaurin is his grandson, Robert.

The Fight: an engraving showing the famous prize fight between Tom Sayers of Great Britain and John C. Heenan of America, which took place on 17 April 1860. The accounts of the event are numerous but one old resident, Mrs M. Ray, pictured opposite, recounted it vividly when interviewed by the local newspaper in 1914; she recalled that the fight was held in the meadow just beyond what is now known as North Farnborough station. The River Blackwater, dividing Hampshire from Surrey, enabled the assembled throng to move hastily across the border to evade the attentions of the Hampshire constabulary, as bare-fist fighting was illegal. Mrs Ray came to Farnborough as a young bride in 1853 and her husband worked as a porter at Farnborough station. She said: 'there was nothing but the old Toll Gates and a nursery garden between the Tumble Down Dick Hotel and the canal bridge on the Farnborough Road, and the site of the nursery garden is now occupied by the Queen's Hotel.'

Mrs M. Ray, aged eighty-one, 1914. She lived for many years in Chapel House, next to the old Primitive Methodist Chapel in Chapel Street, built in 1867. Mrs Ray died in December 1914.

George Hurdle and his daughter, Eliza, c. 1875. Mr Hurdle was a blacksmith in Farnborough Street. Eliza married her father's apprentice, William Bartlett, who, in 1869, opened a blacksmith's in the old schoolhouse in Rectory Road.

The wedding of H.A. 'Gus' Bartlett and Lillian Chandler, 1905. Back row, left to right: William Bartlett, Jessie Bartlett, William Chandler (father of the bride). Seated are William Bartlett, the bridegroom's father, and Mrs Chandler, the bride's mother; the two bridesmaids are Esme Yeomans and Gwen King. Taken in Farnborough Street, next to the Prince of Wales, this photograph features four local families whose names are synonymous with many of the activities of the villages of Farnborough and nearby Cove.

Section Two

THE ARRIVAL OF THE ARMY

Edward VII. This photograph, taken by amateur photographer Tudor Lawrence in about 1906, has captured the obliging mood of the visiting monarch when he turned especially to smile at the camera.

A royal visit, 1905. Edward VII, accompanied by the King of Spain, is departing from Farnborough station on his way to review the troops on Laffan's Plain. In the background, to the right, is the old stationmaster's house and to the left a train is standing in the sidings.

Cove Common, *c.* 1902. This was the view from the Queen's Hotel. The army training camp can be seen here, before the army balloon factory moved to the common in 1905. Just visible in the distance, to the right, are the towers of St Michael's Abbey and Hillside Convent. Between the two men standing in the centre foreground are the tracks for the tram which ran from Farnborough station to the Queen's Hotel; it ceased operation before 1900.

Government House, *c.* 1906. Built in 1883, this imposing house of red brick and stone was the residence of the General Officer Commanding of the army. Situated just off Farnborough Road, to the west of the Queen's Hotel, it overlooked an ornamental lake in 19 acres of grounds known as Cove Park.

The annual military fête in the grounds of Government House, *c.* 1907. This grand event was held here for many years. In this photograph a pushball competition is in progress, and in the background are the swings, roundabouts and sideshows belonging to Redshirt Matthews, of the famous fairground family, whose base was in south Farnborough. The name has been perpetuated in Matthews Close, a small residential development built on the site of their old winter quarters.

The Wesleyan Soldiers' Home, *c.* 1900. Originally built in Aldershot, it was taken down and removed to this site on Lynchford Road, at the top of the Queen's Avenue, in 1875.

Wesleyan Soldiers' Home after it had been greatly enlarged, *c.* 1905. The gate and railings remained, but the central part had been rebuilt, with two turrets added at the side. The building was subsequently renamed the Harrington Home but has now been demolished, and the area has been grassed over and planted with trees.

The Soldiers' Institute before 1900. This was erected opposite the Wesleyan Church in Lynchford Road, to further serve the needs of the nearby soldiers. For many years it bore the words 'Soldiers' Institute' painted in large letters on the roof.

Church of England Soldiers' & Sailors' Institute, *c.* 1907. The small building above was enlarged to accommodate refreshment areas, billiard rooms, baths, and reading and writing rooms, thus reflecting the needs of the ever increasing military population. Now converted into offices and renamed St Alban's House, it lies on an island site adjacent to the roundabout at the south end of Alexandra Road.

A military band marching down Lynchford Road before the First World War. This was a familiar and colourful sight and every Sunday the children would rush to see the soldiers in nearby Queen's Parade, as they practised their marching to and from church services. People would cycle furiously around the area to gain the best vantage points.

Farnborough Common, 1908. Officers in their training encampment can be seen, and in the background are buildings 3 and 29 of the Balloon Factory. A new army airship, Nulli Secundus 2, is being demonstrated.

Young men of Cambridge University Officers' Training Camp attending church service, 1912. As many as three thousand men occupied these camps, necessitating the provision of temporary supplies of water and sanitation facilities. Farnborough Road is in the background.

The Army Aircraft Factory, *c.* 1911. The factory was fast becoming a major employer, with over fifty men and fifty women there in 1909. This increased rapidly as the scope of the factory developed into experimental work, testing of new developments and training of military and aviation personnel.

George V passing through Farnborough to attend the annual review of troops, June 1913. As was usual on those occasions, schools closed to allow the children to welcome the king.

Military signals at North Farnborough. This signal-box was on the Reading to Guildford line, where a long platform enabled troops and horses to disembark. The station is now only in civilian use, with a shorter platform. The signal-box has gone, but still visible are the refurbished gates to the marshalling yards, serving as a reminder of busier times.

EMPRESS EUGÉNIE

*Empress Eugénie, 1880. This photograph was
taken in Cape Town, which she visited while
making a pilgrimage to see the place of her son's
death in the Zulu War.*

Farnborough Hill, *c.* 1900. Empress Eugénie bought the house from the Longman family in 1880 together with the land across the railway, where she built a mausoleum on the hill in memory of her husband, the exiled Emperor Napoleon III of France and her son, the Prince Imperial.

A house on the Farnborough Hill estate, *c.* 1890. Quite a number of the empress' staff lived in accommodation provided on the estate.

Wounded officers at Farnborough Hill, 1914. During the First World War, the empress opened up the annexe as a hospital for wounded English officers. Empress Eugénie is seated centre left and the commandant of the hospital, Lady Haig (wife of General Sir Douglas Haig), is to her right. Behind are Mr and Mrs Long of the empress' staff, Mr Edward Lee and other visitors. The empress was a familiar figure locally, often seen travelling about the village or walking her dog in the grounds across the Farnborough Road, which is now a residential area known as the Empress Estate. Occasionally she would meet the pupils of Hillside Convent, who were allowed to picnic by the lake, another feature now filled in and built upon. The empress also took a great interest in the village school and often gave parties for the poor children of the area, thus continuing the benevolence of her predecessors at Farnborough Hill.

Empress Eugénie's staff at Farnborough Hill. This photograph was probably taken around the turn of the century, and although many of the staff were brought in from further afield there were certainly some local people among them.

The entrance lodge at Farnborough Hill, *c.* 1900. This view from inside the grounds shows the gate on to Farnborough Road. The man standing beside the gate is probably the lodge keeper, who, according to local historian the late Gus Bartlett, 'was very pompous in his high hat and frock coat'.

Another lodge to Farnborough Hill, *c.* 1902. This one is further north along Farnborough Road and was occupied by Mr Lomas, once batman to the Prince Imperial. The gate is now used as the exit to the convent school, which presently occupies the property.

Empress Eugénie's old Renault. A sad end had befallen this green and black striped Renault when it was discovered in a local scrapyard in the late 1930s. On the death of the empress in 1920 the car was inherited by her chauffeur and former coachman and used as a taxi for a while. It was entered in the 1934 carnival by Mr Lascelles, and then, having outlived its usefulness, ended up here.

The arrival of the body of Empress Eugénie at Farnborough station, 1920. The empress died on 11 July at the age of ninety-four, while visiting Spain. Her body was conveyed in state through France and thence to the abbey at Farnborough, where many mourners filed past to pay their last respects.

The empress' funeral, 20 July 1920. Local people turned out in their hundreds to watch the arrival of many visiting dignitaries, including representatives of many of the royal families of Europe. This was the scene outside the Cambridge Hotel, opposite the railway station, near the entrance to the abbey.

Royal mourners at the funeral. Among those departing from the abbey are George V (top hat in hand), Princess Clémentine of Belgium (veiled), the King of Spain (in uniform), the Duke of Connaught (top right, moustached), Princess Beatrix, and the King and Queen of Albania.

The Imperial Crypt at Farnborough Abbey. The empress was buried here alongside the tombs of her husband and son.

THE BIRTH OF
AVIATION

Col. S.F. Cody, who made the first official flight

in an aeroplane in Great Britain, in 1908.

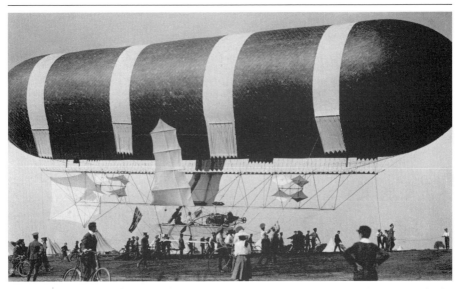

The first military airship. The Nulli Secundus was first flown in 1907, although the original planning was commenced by Col. Templer in 1903. It was made of goldbeater's skin (gut of an ox), and on 5 October 1907, piloted by Col. Capper and S.F. Cody, made a flight to London at an average speed of 16 m.p.h.

The naval airships Beta and Baby. Baby, smaller and cheaper, was 81 ft long, had a two-bladed propeller and was powered by two 8 h.p. engines. Beta was a longer, more advanced version. The goldbeater's skins, used for the envelope, were treated locally by women who were employed to clean and scrape the fat off the animal gut. More than ten layers of skin were then stuck together and stretched across the steel-wire framework.

The airship sheds, 1912. After construction, the left-hand shed was raised 15 ft to accommodate a later airship, the Lebaudy. It is obvious from the assembled crowd that the ever increasing activities on the airfield were attracting much local curiosity.

The Royal Aircraft Factory, 1916. The old army factory was renamed in 1912 and by 1916 it was employing nearly five thousand people, including three thousand women. Apparently the factory was unpopular with some local residents as it caused a great shortage of domestic servants in the area.

The Lebaudy airship, 1911. This was damaged when it hit the low roof of the airship shed. The roof was subsequently raised, and the airship is seen here, after repairs, coming out of the building. Also visible at the side of the shed is an air balloon, the forerunner of these huge airships.

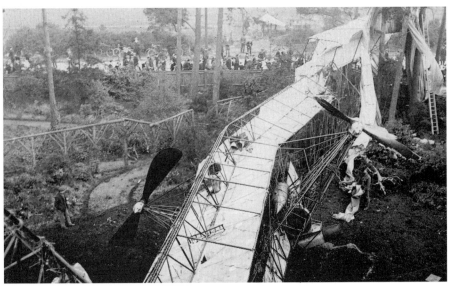

Disaster strikes. On its test flight on 4 May 1911, the repaired Lebaudy went out of control and missed its mooring. The trailropes dragged across the trees beside Farnborough Road and the airship collapsed on to Woodlands Cottage, draping its envelope over the roof and garden.

The disaster drew many spectators. Miraculously, nobody was hurt, but people rushed to the scene to view the tangled mess of steel and rubber fabric (which had taken the place of skins to make the envelope). Despite the efforts of the local constabulary several pieces of this new rubber fabric were removed by spectators as mementos. The house, owned by Col. Jessop, was not seriously damaged and although at first the owners of the airship denied liability, eventually their insurers agreed to pay for the repairs. A local builder was employed and the bill, which included work to the roof, chimneys, upstairs walls and balcony, came to £54 9s 9d. There was, in fact, more damage to the garden, where six large fir trees were destroyed, and it cost £54 17s 6d to replace the trees, shrubs, flowers and lawns. The site is now occupied by the old Farnborough Telephone Exchange.

Col. Cody's first aeroplane. The first official flight in an aeroplane in Great Britain was made by Cody over Farnborough in 1908. The original plane crashed but was repaired and modified, and is seen here in around 1910 beside a shed rented from the balloon factory.

SCENE OF COL. CODY'S ACCIDENT.

Col. Cody's fatal accident, 1913. He was killed while making a test flight on Laffan's Plain in a new biplane, which he was going to enter in the *Daily Mail* Race around Britain. His passenger, Hampshire cricketer, W.H.B. Evans, also died in the crash.

Funeral of The late Col: Cody
The Worlds Greatest Airman.
Aldershot. Aug. 11th 1913

The funeral of Samuel Franklin Cody, on 11 August 1913. He was born in Texas in 1861 and after much travelling came to England with his family in 1890 and became a professional entertainer. He came to Aldershot in 1904 where he began his new career in aviation. His courage and tenacity helped him to develop aviation, from kiteflying to balloons and from thence to airships and eventually aeroplanes. His home was in Ash Vale and he was buried at Aldershot Cemetery. The procession, which included famous aviators, members of parliament, all the members of the Royal Flying Corps, and representatives of every corps in the military command, is seen here crossing the railway at North Camp station on its way along Lynchford Road. The whole of the 2½ mile route was lined with crowds of people.

Marching along Lynchford Road, the funeral procession passes the junction of Peabody Road. Curtains were drawn along the route and most of the shops in Farnborough and Aldershot closed as a mark of respect.

COL. S. F. CODY, Deceased.

.. CATALOGUE ..

OF THE

Contents of the

AIRCRAFT WORKS

LAFFAN'S PLAIN, ALDERSHOT

WHICH

MESSRS.

KINGHAM & KINGHAM

Will Sell by Auction, on

MONDAY, SEPTEMBER 8th, 1913

at 12 o'clock precisely.

SOLICITORS :
Messrs. AMERY, PARKES & Co.,
18, Fleet Street, London, E.C.

Following Col. Cody's death, all his aircraft accessories and equipment were sold. The catalogue contained 211 lots.

There was a great deal of interest shown in the sale, which took place in the actual shed in which Col. Cody used to build his machines. Edgar Kingham was the auctioneer and in the crowd were Grahame White, the famous aviator, and the Revd Basil Phillips, vicar of St Mark's, who himself had made some local flights. The interesting array of articles included engines, wings, rudders, tyres, bits of steel tubing, a Singer sewing-machine and even bamboo poles – all the essential parts to build an early aeroplane! After very keen bidding, one of Cody's monoplanes fetched £14, a glider went for £4 10s, but an ingenious new design of propeller raised £7 because it had only been used on a couple of occasions. All 211 lots were sold, including this large shed, containing a workshop and office.

An army monoplane, *c.* 1913. All the early flying machines were a source of interest and curiosity to the local people, who often gathered to watch when a flight was imminent.

The Royal Flying Corps barracks, *c.* 1917. After 1918 these were used by the Royal Air Force. T.E. Lawrence (Lawrence of Arabia) spent a couple of months here in 1922 while stationed in the RAF School of Photography. Situated opposite Netley Street on Farnborough Road, it is now hostel accommodation.

The headquarters of the Royal Flying Corps, 1917. Situated opposite Aircraft Esplanade on Farnborough Road, it was occupied by the RAF on its formation in 1918.

ROYAL AIRCRAFT FACTORY
PLANNING DEPT.

FROM EARLY MORN
TILL LATE AT NIGHT
"DELIVERING GOODS"
BUT MERRY & BRIGHT.

A team of swimmers, *c.* 1916. This group of young men in typical swimwear of the period could well have been a team representing the Planning Department in some local sports competition.

Royal Aircraft Establishment sports day, early 1920s. These spectators are enjoying a day out on the RAE sports ground, which, until the Second World War, was situated on the south side of Hillside Convent, on Farnborough Road, approximately where the National Remote Sensing Centre is today.

The main entrance to the RAE, mid-1920s. This entrance opposite Boundary Road is now called North Gate and looks somewhat different today; it is used mainly as an exit gate at busy times. The old RAE Assembly Halls are on the left.

TRANSPORT

The Farnborough miniature railway.

South Farnborough Working Men's Club, *c.* 1924. Among those off to Southsea in the charabanc, which was restricted to 12 m.p.h., are ? Piercey, Bert Scivier, C. Yeoman, Sid Roberts, Harry Roberts, Percy Pancott, F. Roberts, ? Wilkinson, ? Heath and ? Collins.

A royal visit, *c.* 1903. This open carriage was often used when royalty came by train to inspect the troops on Laffan's Plain. Hundreds of people would line the route and, as can be seen, the photographers with their paraphernalia would take up vantage points on the stable roof of the Railway Hotel, now the Ham and Blackbird.

Farnborough Road, near the railway station, *c.* 1904. Carriages, horses and bicycles were the general mode of transport then, but just visible on the left are the remains of the tram tracks used when horse-drawn trams ran along Farnborough Road to the Queen's Hotel.

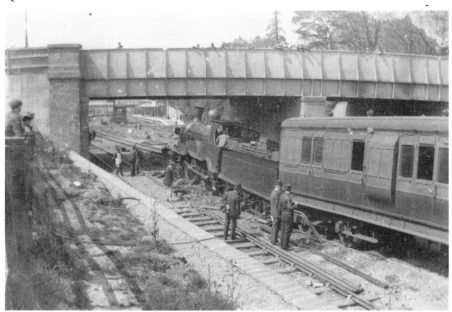

A railway mishap, 1904. The engine seems to have come off the track while widening work was in progress just beneath the bridge outside Farnborough station. The damage does not look very serious, but the accident attracted spectators from the bridge above, as well as a small boy with his dog up on the left embankment.

Farnborough L&SWR station, *c.* 1910. The demolition of the old stationmaster's house has left a large forecourt, much needed with the increased use of the railway. A variety of taxis lined up on the left and an open-topped omnibus await the arrival of the next train, but a lone horse and cart still has its place as a means of transport.

An RAE steamroller in front of one of the earliest buildings in the RAE, 1919.

One of the RAE locomotives with the airship sheds in the background, 1919.

The *Invincible*. Until 1968 the RAE had its own railway, which ran along Elm Grove Road and across Victoria Road, taking goods from the railway station into the RAE. Many will remember the man walking in front with a red flag, held up to stop the traffic. Originally, steam traction engines were used, before the first steam locomotive was brought in from the Royal Ordnance Factory at Woolwich. The line was built by prisoners in the First World War and at one time it was carrying over 12,000 tons of freight a year. The only reminders today are a couple of yards of track beside the garages at the junction of Elm Grove Road and Union Street and the name of Invincible Road, which runs along much of the route of the old railway. The *Invincible* was retired to the Isle of Wight for use on a passenger railway.

The Farnborough miniature railway. Charles Bullock, who lived in Prospect Avenue, built a miniature railway on land known as Foxhills, which was leased from Grange Farm. It was opened to the public in 1936. Here, Dr Bernard is the engine driver.

This photograph featured in an advertisement offering 1 mile round trips for 6*d* (children half price). Such was its popularity that car-parking and teas were offered to the crowds who came when it was open on Wednesdays, Saturdays and Sundays.

A signal-box in miniature. Mr Bullock teamed up with Alexander Davenport Kinloch, who eventually took over the running of the railway. He is seen here in the fully equipped signal-box. In 1939 the railway closed, having given rides to thousands of people who had enjoyed this new form of entertainment on their doorstep.

North Camp station before 1923. The sign at the station on the Reading to Guildford line advised passengers to change here for Ash Vale and South Farnborough. The troops disembarking here created many a grand spectacle, marching along past the shops in Lynchford Road to their barracks.

The crossroads by the Clockhouse, 1930s. Cars and buses had become a common sight along Farnborough Road, past the junction with Rectory and Salisbury Roads. Brand's furniture removers occupy the building on the corner, which has now been replaced by the modern glass offices of Concept 2000.

Booth & Jacob furniture removers. These vans, seen here at the company depository in Queen's Road, were a familiar sight locally.

RELIGION

St Mark's Vicarage, 1909. The Revd Basil Phillips
is seen here, probably with his family. Many fêtes
and fund-raising garden parties were held in the
vicarage grounds. The building has since been
demolished, to be replaced by St Mark's Close.

Farnborough parish church, *c.* 1908. This has been the site of a church for over a thousand years. The seventeenth-century tower is built of ships' timbers and the wooden porch is thirteenth century. The lychgate was erected in 1907 by Harold Holt in memory of his parents, Maj. and Mrs Holt of Farnborough Grange.

The Old Rectory, *c.* 1906. Built in around 1830 and now a private residence, it stands near the junction of Abbey Way and Rectory Road. The hymn 'There is a Green Hill Far Away' by Mrs Alexander is reputed to have been written here and inspired by the parish church on the hill, which was felt to be reminiscent of the hill of Calvary outside Jerusalem.

Farnborough campanologists. This group of handbell ringers is pictured outside the parish church in 1901; it soon disbanded because too much time was taken up in practising. D. McLaurin is on the extreme right.

The parish church choir, 1901. Back row, left to right: H.A. Bartlett, T. Tottle, G. Bennett, W. Russell, T. Joyce; third row: W. Weller, D. Spooner, G. Strickland, N. Spooner, W. Lowe; second row: W. Bickerstaff, E. Golder (headmaster), E. McLaurin, Revd A.E. Kinch (rector), J. Bridger (organist), E. Lee, J. Bennett; front row: J. Lucas, R. Goodall, F. Bartlett, A. Bennett, R. Cresswell, W. Lawrence.

FARNBOROUGH. — Abbey Church

St Michael's Abbey and Imperial Mausoleum, *c*. 1900. They were built by Empress Eugénie as a memorial to her late husband. Her son and the empress herself are also buried there.

The monastery at St Michael's Abbey, *c*. 1895. This large red-brick and stone building was erected by Empress Eugénie and first occupied by a community of Premonstratensian monks. On their departure, the Benedictine monks arrived from France. The clock in the tower was made by the same individual as the one in Farnborough Clockhouse and is still in good working order, handwound every day by the monks.

The extension to the monastery, *c*. 1900. Requiring more room, the monks commissioned this tower to be built in stone. One of the novice monks, Benedict Williamson, designed the new building, which was similar in style to the monastery they had occupied in France.

An aerial view of St Michael's Abbey and the monastery, *c*. 1920. The railway is hidden in the cutting below the trees and beyond is Highgate Lane and the grounds of Farnborough Hill, whose driveway can be seen top left.

A presentation at the abbey, *c*. 1920. Maréchal Pétain of France is presenting a war medal to Dom Godu, one of the monks who served in the First World War. Abbot Cabrol is in the front, Dom Godu is third from right, and fourth from right is Dom du Boisruvray, who became abbot following the death of Abbot Cabrol.

St Mark's Church, south Farnborough, *c*. 1909. Building commenced in 1881 and was completed in 1896, at a cost of £5,000, defrayed by public subscription. Built to ease the pressure on the parish church, it served much of the military area of North Camp.

St Mark's Memorial, *c.* 1925. The memorial was first erected in front of the church in honour of those who gave their lives in the First World War. It now stands in front of the church hall, between Alexandra Road and Guildford Road.

The Gospel Tabernacle, 1905. Built by Pastor Rawlings on the corner of Queen's Road and York Road, this later became the Farnborough Baptist church. Like all the churches in this area it served an expanding population with military influences, and had a very active congregation of followers and a well-attended Sunday school.

Broomfield House, *c.* 1900. For some time this house, which stands at the southern end of Alexandra Road, next to the Methodist church, was the residence of the Wesleyan minister. Now devoid of trees and the neat front hedge, it is used as offices.

Wesleyan Methodist church, *c.* 1900. Built in the 1880s to serve a predominantly military population, it remains much the same today but without the chimneys and turret. Next door is the church day school attended by local children until Queen's Road Council School was built in 1912. The church school building still stands but is now hidden by Lloyds Bank.

Section Seven

EDUCATION

Queen's Road Council School, mid-1930s.

Group I at the National School, north Farnborough, *c.* 1907. Miss Beck is the teacher on the right, Miss Buss is on the left and the little boy in a sailor suit (third row, second from right) is Cecil Gosney.

Standard IV, Farnborough Street School, 1920. Back row, left to right: Henry Bilby, ? Baxter, Ernie Vince, Bill Miles, Bill Cooper, George Paul, Ralph Woods; third row: Doris Hedger, -?-, ? Ede, ? Ede, Maggie McCully, ? Lucas, Miss Hoyes; second row: -?-, Annie Hulcup, -?-, Muriel Parr, Minnie Watson, Grace Stillwell, Florrie Swain; front row: Fred Paul, Reg Coleman, Austen Gosney, ? Sharland, Les Hammond, -?-.

The National Children's Home, 1906. It was built in 1898 on Alexandra Road, in 2½ acres of grounds, and provided accommodation for one hundred boys. The school band was a regular sight on Sunday, marching along Alexandra Road to church. Later it became Council offices, before being demolished and replaced by flats now known as Wetherby Gardens.

Afternoon tea at the children's home, c. 1908. This was an orphanage as well as a home for youngsters who had been committed under the Industrial Schools Act. The photograph shows the staff trying to create a family atmosphere within the home.

Queen's Road Council School, mid-1930s. Mr Miller, at the back, was the first headmaster when the school opened in 1912. Also pictured are Maisie Roberts, Audrey Harris, Peter Roberts, Harold Hogsflesh, Mabel Bartholomew, Betty Holloway, ? O'Shaunessy, Elsie Mason, Madeleine Poulter, Joyce Crisp, Bobby Jeans, Peter Robinson and Alma Dunn.

Champion border schools, 1936. Being situated on the county border, local schools participated in athletics competitions with nearby Surrey schools. Pupils of Queen's Road School won the boys' and girls' championship shields in a number of sports that year, and the competitors are seen here with their trophies.

Salesian School, 1912. Opened in Queen's Road as a diocesan orphanage by the Salesian Fathers in 1901, it then became a regular boarding school for boys, offering a religious, classical and commercial education.

St Mark's School, c. 1916. The pupils are dressed as minstrels for a show which was probably put on to raise money for the war effort. To the left are Mr Barker, the headmaster, and his wife, while the Revd Basil Phillips is to the right.

Hillside on Star Hill, 1889. This house was purchased by the nuns of the Congregation of Christian Education and opened as a boarding school on 15 May 1889, primarily for daughters of army officers stationed locally. Seated on the bench to the right are Mme Caroline Murray, a founder nun, and her sister Mme de Villalonga. The three pupils on the grass are Susanna and Josephine Murray, nieces of Mme Caroline, with a French pupil, Marie Marjorie, between them. The smaller house in the grounds was later opened as a day school. In 1893 a large extension was built, incorporating a central clocktower and chapel. The imposing building in the top picture opposite became Hillside College, and continued to be used by the nuns even after they purchased Farnborough Hill. Eventually it was sold to the RAE in 1945. There was a short period during the First World War when the premises were commandeered by the War Office and it became known as Star Hill Barracks. It has been recently refurbished and turned into a smart, modern office block but in the process the original house was demolished and replaced by an extension presumably designed to look symmetrical with the chapel. The bottom picture opposite shows St Mary's Day School, also built by the nuns in 1899 on land directly across the road from Hillside.

Hillside College and chapel (right), 1900. The college extension almost dwarfs the original house on the left. It was designed by Mr Hansom the elder, whose family was credited with the design of the hansom cab; the same architect was responsible for St Mary's Day School.

St Mary's Day School, 1900. This photograph is taken from inside the gates of Hillside. In 1926 the building was sold and became Farnborough Secondary School.

Farnborough Secondary School 1st XI, 1926. Back row, left to right: Mr L. Besanvalle, A. Gosney, A. Baverstock, H. Watson, R. Knight (vice-capt.), W. Leeming (capt.), Mr R.H. May; second row: G. Colvin, W. Sinden, W. Halsey, K. Saunders, W. Harris; front: L. Barnett. The school was situated at the junction of Sycamore Road and Farnborough Road. The adjacent properties, set in the pine-clad surroundings of Farnborough Road, Boundary Road, and Albert Road, were well suited to educational use. The proximity to the pine woods was considered healthy, and the playing fields were ideal because the soil conditions allowed heavy rain to drain away quickly.

St Mark's football team, 1924/5. Back row, left to right: E. Parr, W. Croft, J. Spreadborough, E. Thomas, H. Thorn, M. Flatt; front row: E. Guest, A. Drury, ? Yeomans, W. Perkiss, J. Parsons.

Farnborough School, *c.* 1906. This impressive building, formerly Castledon Hall, was a preparatory school for about one hundred boys. The building was demolished after the Second World War and the site is now occupied by Farnborough College of Technology.

The swimming pool at Farnborough School, 1907. The school had excellent sporting facilities; its playing fields were on land across Farnborough Road, access to which was via a tunnel. The swimming pool was attached to the main building.

Belgrave House School, 1922. This school catered for boys aged seven to fifteen who were to go on to public school or the Royal Naval College at Dartmouth. Now demolished, it was next to the grounds of Farnborough School, on the opposite corner of Sycamore Road from St Mary's Day School.

Pinewood School, c. 1930. Another preparatory school, this was in Albert Road and was the scene of many memorable cricket matches. Plays and pageants were performed here, which were very popular with the local people. During the Second World War the school transferred to the West Country. The building was then used as a furniture depository by Brand's removals, before its subsequent demolition.

Section Eight

PEOPLE AT WORK

Delivering bread to the troops, early 1900s.

Delivering the post, *c*. 1915. Miss Jessie Bartlett is seen here delivering on the Marlborough Lines. She later married the postmaster, Mr Tulip.

The fire brigade, *c*. 1900. This was formed in about 1899 and consisted of volunteer firemen. Their captain, Mr Fitch, is seated centre and immediately behind him is D. McLaurin.

William Fitch, captain of the fire brigade, seen here at the Cambridge Hotel near Farnborough railway station, *c.* 1905. Mr Fitch was Chief Gymnastic Instructor of the Royal Military College from 1888 until he retired in 1893. As a civilian he taught at Farnborough School, Belgrave School and Hillside, as well as giving private tuition in fencing to the Duke of Connaught's children at their home in Government House, Farnborough.

Delivering to the troops, early 1900s. Mr Cassidy is conveying bread from Mr Chitty's shop in Peabody Road.

Farnborough police station, *c.* 1910. This ivy-clad building in Lynchford Road, adjacent to what is now the NatWest Bank, was demolished after the police moved to their present building in Pinehurst Avenue. The sergeant-in-charge was William James Onsell.

Local constabulary caught in the act, *c.* 1910. Cleaning up the town or drunk in charge? The reason for their antics is not known but perhaps they should be on the other side of the bars.

Mr Gough, master carpenter, *c.* 1900. This lectern is being made by Mr Gough for a local church. He was also one of the carpenters who worked on the construction of the Clockhouse on Farnborough Road.

Down on the farm, 1930s. Much of the land to the north and west of the town was being farmed until the Second World War. Here it is haymaking time on Grange Farm, tenanted by the Oakey family, who originally came to the town at the turn of the century to grow strawberries but did not find the growing conditions to be suitable. They turned to dairy farming and also took over the tenancy of Whitehall and Southwood farms for a time. Along with certain other local farmers they were accorded the right to cut hay from Farnborough Common, which now forms part of the RAE. The rick-building is being carried out here with the aid of a power-driven elevator but the horse is still a very important part of the agricultural scene.

Cutting hay on the common, 1938. Ernest Oakey is seen here on the first tractor to be used on his farms. Following the outbreak of war in 1939, the land was requisitioned for military use and Southwood Camp was built here.

Grange Farm milk cart, 1935. Young Walter Oakey, nephew of Ernest, is seen here on one of the carts used for milk delivery from the Grange Farm Dairy in Alexandra Road.

A.J. 'Digger' Armstrong in RAF uniform, c. 1920. Mr Armstrong, a well-known local figure now in his nineties, joined the Royal Flying Corps which later became the Royal Air Force. He is seen here on leave just before going back into 'civvie street'.

RAE apprentices, early 1920s. 'Digger' Armstrong, front row centre, joined the Royal Aircraft Factory in 1913 as a trade lad, and ultimately became the apprentice master. He saw many famous service personnel pass through his workshops. Now the oldest surviving apprentice, he was awarded the MBE in 1965. Also in the photograph are Percy Johnson and Tom Poulter.

Yeoman's Tilbury Mineral Water Works, one of four local bottling plants, occupied a site at the top end of Queen's Road, where CMS Carpets now has its premises. Above, a stone mineral water bottle, *c.* 1900; below, one of their advertisements.

Until 1914 the fire brigade only had a horse-drawn vehicle. Then a motorized vehicle was purchased for £850, despite fierce local opposition. This took the form of local protest meetings and petitions, while correspondence in the local newspaper indicated people's outrage at the 'unjustifiable' expense. Proficiency competitions were held regularly and there was keen rivalry among the local brigades. From reports in the newspapers of the time, Farnborough appears to have done well in those early years. Here, in 1924, the trophy winners pose outside their headquarters at the Town Hall; they include John Shaw, Bert Lay, P. Smith and C. Englefield.

SHOPPING
FACILITIES

Thomas White & Co., 1922. This busy scene outside the department store in Lynchford Road illustrates a thriving shopping area, at the time considered to be the best for miles around. The scene is much changed today as the falling demands of a decreasing military population have brought a corresponding decline in shopping facilities.

Victoria Road looking east, *c*. 1930. In the foreground are the tracks of the old *Invincible* railway. Wright the outfitter is on the corner of Elmgrove Road and further along is Williamsons the grocer. On the right, with its doors open, is Spooner's forge, with Landymore's confectioner's next door. Today office buildings line the road as far as the eye can see. As the population grew, particularly in the south of the town, Lynchford Road on the edge of North Camp became the main shopping area. The needs of other parts of the town were served by a few shops and businesses in Victoria Road and along Farnborough Road. The emphasis has now shifted to the shopping malls of the Kingsmead, Queensmead and Princes Mead complex, built nearby.

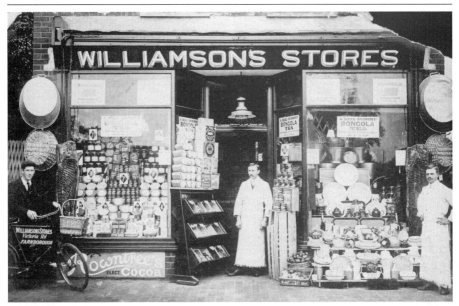

Williamsons in Victoria Road, *c*. 1909. This provisions store was licensed to sell tobacco and patent medicines as well as stocking an excellent line in special blends of tea. A daily delivery service was also offered to the customer.

Landymore, tobacconist and confectioner, Victoria Road, 1937. The flags are up outside Charlie Landymore's shop to celebrate the coronation of George VI.

Gibson & Jory's drapery shop in Victoria Road, *c.* 1910. Miss Gibson is on the left and Miss Jory is on the right. Today it is the site of the Royal Bank of Scotland.

Pinehurst Corner, early 1920s. Situated opposite the entrance to Oak Road, this popular little café and shop were pulled down in the 1970s to make way for road improvements. A car-park now stands on the site.

Aircraft Esplanade, *c*. 1920. Its name is indicative of its proximity to the early aircraft factory. This little row of shops on Farnborough Road would have served the factory workers as well as the many new houses being built in the surrounding area of south Farnborough.

The post office, south Farnborough, 1920s. On the corner of Netley Street and Alexandra Road, it served the area until the new post office was built near the Town Hall in the late 1930s. The house has been demolished and the land is now used for the sale of cars.

Mrs Chitty is seen here with her daughter and niece outside their shop at 140 Peabody Road, *c.* 1914. The shop was later taken over by the Goble family.

E. Grenham beside Sheldon's three-wheeled delivery van, 1935. The Alton Ale Stores, in Queen's Road, is now called Sheldon's and is still a family-run bakery today.

The shop occupied by the Lloyd family, 1909. Now part of Howard's the newsagent, it has slightly different windows but is still recognizable.

DON'T WAIT AND SEE! COME NOW AND SEE *Our New Branch* **CAMP ROAD FARNBORO'**

This postcard was an advertisement for the new branch of the Co-op, opened some time before 1915. The building is no longer a Co-op, but the words 'No. 1 Branch Farnborough' remain today to remind us of the times when many of the nationally known shops had branches in the town.

Mr Chapman's shop in Camp Road, 1923. Milk stout was one of the new drinks recently introduced by Simonds, whose local branch was in Farnborough Street. There, even today, a Simonds' hop leaf can be seen on one of the old buildings.

Luncheons and teas were served in many establishments as a secondary part of a shop. Here, C. Berry combines a teashop with the bakery business, next door to the YMCA building in Camp Road, 1923. It is now occupied by a taxi company.

Home & Colonial, 1920s. This national company was on the corner of Camp Road and Lynchford Road; Boots the Cash Chemist was next door, and Maypole and the International Stores were further down Lynchford Road. The open-top omnibus of the Aldershot & District Traction Company is about to turn into Queen's Avenue.

Frisby's shoe shop, next to North Camp Hotel on Lynchford Road, *c.* 1920. How about buying a new pair of boots for 5s 11d? Shoe repairs cost 1s 6d.

The pavements are crowded with shoppers at the junction of Queen's Avenue and Lynchford Road, 1920s. Notice how everybody, including the lady riding the bicycle, is wearing a hat, even for shopping.

Mr Millard outside his shop, The Busy Bee Stores, in 1923. This was also Lynchford Road post office and, as the sign over the shop proclaims, he was a well-known local tea blender.

Mr Hyde worked in Frisby's before opening at 10 Market Place, photographed in around 1923. The pavement along this stretch of Lynchford Road was wide enough for market stalls.

The Bon Marché, 1923. There was something for all the family at this fancy goods shop next door to Hyde's.

'Along the Front', early 1930s. Lynchford Road looked out across the Camp and with shops on one side only, the locals likened it to the seafront. This view looks down Lynchford Road from the junction with Peabody Road. There have been many changes; today the corn stores has been replaced by a florist and many of the shops further down are motor cycle and car sales showrooms, though the building next to Turners is still a hairdresser's. The signpost behind the railings on the right points towards a Methodist Church, which was in Peabody Road. The gas street lamps on the corner were replaced by electric lighting in 1935, when Lynchford Road was one of only four roads in the town to benefit from this more modern form of illumination.

Market Place, Lynchford Road, *c.* 1905. On the far right, next to Senior's newsagent's, is the early Primitive Methodist church, later to become Ranger's furnishings' store. Yates' corn stores is visible on the far left, but comparison with the previous photograph will show that the tall building to its right, the hairdresser's, originally had a flat roof.

An attractive row of Victorian shops called The Pavement, *c.* 1912. The sign on the left entreats the traffic to drive slowly, which is evidence of the ever increasing volume of traffic passing along Lynchford Road to the Camp.

Along Lynchford Road there were five boot and shoe shops within a quarter of a mile. Here, Dacombe's is in the foreground and another branch of Frisby's is in the distance, *c.* 1910. Beyond Dacombe's is the home and estate office of land developer H.J.E. Brake, where the first meeting of the Farnborough Urban District Council was held on 27 January 1896, before the Town Hall was built.

Another attractive row of houses which is little changed today, *c.* 1905. This is further down Lynchford Road towards North Camp station and beyond Gravel Road. The sign for Johnson's estate agent's can be seen on the centre house, behind the people on the pavement.

Section Ten

LEISURE

ACTIVITIES

*Miss E.D. Vinson of the 1st Farnborough Girl
Guides, 1917. Photographed in the grounds of
St Mark's Vicarage, Miss Vinson, a local
schoolteacher and founder of the Guides in
Farnborough, is proudly holding the first colours
presented to the company.*

North Camp Cycling Club, *c.* 1890. Many of these very energetic gentlemen were local shopkeepers. From left to right: C. Yates, A.E. Fox, W.H. Melhuish, W.C. Dacombe, A.G. Melhuish, T.J. Wilkes, J.A. Bew, H. Brown, Mr Greenwood.

1st Farnborough Boys' Brigade, 1913. Seated in the second row are Officer Treadgold (fifth from left), then Revd Mr Colson and Mr Golder. Front row, left to right: Sidney Gosney, -?-, Harold Gosney, Billy Wiskin, Phil Thoday, Arthur Crutchley, Arthur McCully, ? Wiskin, Cecil Gosney, Pat Jones, -?-, -?-. Left of the flag, at the back, is Edwin Gosney and second from the right, back row, is Arthur Gosney.

1st Farnborough Guides. Together with Miss Vinson, Mrs Croft Watts, wife of a local doctor, and Miss Green formed the company; here, Miss Vinson is in the third row, fourth from left, and Miss Green is third from right.

Bill Bartlett, King's Scout, *c.* 1920. The Scouts were also well established in Farnborough and in 1921 Chief Scout Baden-Powell came to inspect a combined parade of local Scouts and Guides.

The Duke of Connaught inspecting a parade of the St John Ambulance Brigade in Queen's Road, opposite the end of York Road, *c.* 1931. The duke was on a visit to see the demolition of the old wooden church hall and iron room. However, several years passed before the new building was erected, to provide community facilities for the local people. Now it has been converted into a bakery for Sheldon's. In the photograph are Messrs W. Croft, Thomas, Gaines, Clifford and Robinson. The name of the smart Red Cross lady is not known.

The finish of the Farnborough Cycling Club Open '25', 1930. The Farnborough Cycling Club was formed by Alf Rumble and the members were very keen competitors. At the finish of this race along Farnborough Road the timekeepers are seated in front of the telegraph pole, with Mrs Rumble standing to the right.

The RAE Dramatic Society in a performance of *The Two Gentlemen of Soho*, 1929. Before the days of television, public entertainment was provided by groups such as this one, attached to the RAE but open to others in the town. From left to right: Mr Ormerod, Cissie Marchant, -?-, -?-, Mrs Crowfoot, Mr Illingsworth, Phyllis Neale, P. Ferguson.

RAE Operatic Society performers from *HMS Pinafore*, 1931. Pictured are Bobbie Day, Mrs Fenn, Cissie Marchant and Phyllis Neale.

The RAE Operatic Society in *Yeomen of the Guard*, 1939. The flourishing society was formed in 1920 and first performed in the RAE Concert Hall. When this was demolished, performances were put on in Farnborough Town Hall, where this photograph was taken. From left to right: Sid Turner, H. Lockwood, Lorna Bishop, Douglas Churchill, Rebecca Coulter, Laurie Hall, A. Tomlinson, Albert Owen, Wyn Murray, William Nicholson, Florence Midwood, E. Webster, H. Hunt.

Miss Dacombe's concerts, early 1930s. This younger group is participating in one of Miss Dacombe's concerts, which were held in the hall at the rear of the YMCA building in Camp Road. Miss Dacombe is seated in the centre; behind, to the right, is Edna Hurst and Connie Rumble is holding the hoop. Barbara Sheldon, in a flowered dress, is third from left.

3rd Farnborough Guides, 1934. Back row, left to right: Capt. Joan Neale, Vera Hutchings, May Tutt, Dorothy Bentley, -?-, Phyllis Tye, Madge Tibble, Joan Towers, Phyllis Towers, Dorothy Tutt, Joan Parrott (company leader). Front row: -?-, -?-, -?-, Pat Henderson, -?-, -?-, Gladys Hedger, -?-, June Scott, -?-, -?-, -?-, Joan Coney.

The Carnival Queen and attendants. In 1934 Farnborough held its first carnival, with the proceeds going towards an extension and improvements to the local hospital. A whole week was taken up with events, including a procession, children's fancy dress and sports, fun football, displays, competitions, musical events and dances. Back row, left to right: Phyllis Humphreys, Margaret Walker, Therese Card, -?-; seated: Joan Hewitt, Enid Chadd (Carnival Queen), Muriel Sherwood. The pageboy to the left is Derek Hall.

The Baby Show at the carnival. Over a thousand babies, from as far away as Alton and Southampton, were entered. The four judges, Drs Forsythe, Hunter Dunn, Walker and Attenborough, must have had a very difficult task to pick out the winner, seen here with the Carnival Queen.

Robin Hood and his Merry Men, 1934. The Ancient Order of Foresters are seen here with their float in Farnborough Street, before joining the carnival procession. Those taking part were J.W.C. Lucas, Miss J. Bartlett, R. Dancey, H.A. Bartlett, W.F. Hall, Miss F.S. Andrewartha, Miss L.M. Bartlett, R.C. Hermon, J.G. Brown, J. Randall, E. Paul, C. Gosney, F. Paul and H. Hockley, S. Holloway and Miss P. Allum.

The carnival procession, 1935. In the second annual carnival a beautifully decorated float, entered by a local nursery, is seen passing Tottles shop in Peabody Road.

An ox roast, 1935. As part of the silver jubilee celebrations for George V, a fair was held on the Lower Field of Knellwood Estate, now King George V Playing Fields. Frank Tyler came all the way from Stratford-on-Avon to supervise the roasting of an ox.

The Motor Cycle Club, 1930s. There are cloth caps and boaters but not a helmet to be seen on this group lined up behind the houses in Peabody Road.

North Farnborough cricket team, winners of the Hospital Cricket League from 1937 to 1939. Back row: F.D. Jones, P. Willey, H. Porter, W. Gale, G. Lancaster, B. Snuggs, J.W. Morrish; middle row: B. Lancaster, W.E. Bartlett (vice-captain), R. Woods (captain), H.A. Bartlett, C. Spooner; front row: J. Seddon, G. Beeston.

Jubilee Hall Club outing, 1924. There will be many familiar faces in this group. Among them are the McLaurin family, bottom left, and the Colemans, Lloyds and Allums, to name but a few.

The Golf Links, Farnborough Common, *c.* 1913. The houses and shops along Farnborough Road had a good view over the golf course on the common, where gorse still grew in abundance.

Sunday on the common. This snapshot of young Ray Gibbens and his cousin in the late 1930s, with the aircraft factory in the background, is a reminder of the time when an enjoyable afternoon could be spent on the common, looking at all the aeroplanes.

Section Eleven

STREETS AND BUILDINGS

Wilmot House, 1950s. Situated in Union Street,

formerly Workhouse Lane, it was built as the workhouse

for the poor of Yateley, Farnborough and Hartley

Wintney. It ceased to be used as such in the mid-

nineteenth century and was demolished in the early

1980s.

Coleford Bridge, 1914. The lane to Mytchett, just off Rectory Road, led over this bridge across the River Blackwater. Wild flowers abounded in summer, but the low lying meadowlands often flooded on to the road in winter, causing children to miss their schooling. The new Blackwater Valley relief road now runs through the area.

The Grange, 1940s. Originally a small Victorian house built by Mr Timms, the enlarged building became the residence of Maj. Joseph Holt, when it stood in a park surrounded by an estate of about 300 acres. Later used as a hostel for many years, it was eventually demolished to make way for housing. Its lodge still stands on Farnborough Road, opposite the Ship public house.

The Lodge, Farnborough Road, *c.* 1930. Built in around 1820 by Mrs Foreman of Windmill Hill for her nephew Mr Greene, it was originally called The Pavilion. Today it lies hidden in the trees behind the station. Mr Greene's contribution to education in Farnborough is commemorated by Greene's School Lane, where he founded his schools.

Farnborough station before 1871. This photograph, reproduced from *Woking to Southampton* (Middleton Press), shows the original, smaller station, which had just two platforms. When Queen Victoria first came by train to the area to review the troops there was no station at Aldershot so she had to use Farnborough, which is probably why such a grand station was built here.

The Jubilee Hall, *c.* 1900. It was built almost opposite the entrance to the station by Maj. Holt to commemorate Queen Victoria's diamond jubilee in 1897. Next door was the post office. Both buildings have now been replaced by an office block.

Kingsmead and Queensmead, Victoria Road, *c.* 1925. These names are familiar even today, as the houses were pulled down to make way for the Queensmead shopping area, later to be enlarged by the addition of Kingsmead.

The Clockhouse, *c*. 1920. Originally built as a private residence, in 1933 it was bought by Alfred Pearson, the founder of Pearson's estate agency, who converted a couple of ground-floor rooms to offices. It had the distinction of having the telephone number Farnborough 1. The large room just beneath the clocktower was used as a tea room during the early 1940s. It is still in use as an estate agency but the belltower has been lowered by about 6 ft. In the distance are the buildings occupied by Brand's removals but these have long since gone, to be replaced by the great glass offices of Concept 2000. Today, as one negotiates the busy Clockhouse roundabout, it is hard to imagine the time when only a couple of bicycles interrupted the photographer's view of this local landmark.

The lodge gates, *c.* 1925. These two little lodge gates, which stood at the junction of Rectory Road and Farnborough Road, opposite the Clockhouse, were originally the entrance to Farnborough Place but were demolished when part of Farnborough Park was sold for housing.

Salisbury Road, *c.* 1930. Today there are usually many more cars parked here on the road leading up towards the parish church. The right-hand corner looks much the same but more recent developments now obscure the view of the present rectory.

Farnborough Place, 1936. The present building, now occupied by St Peter's Junior School, dates from the reign of Queen Anne, and for over three hundred years it was the home of the lords of the manor. In 1936, like many of the big old houses in the town, it was being used as a hotel, 'especially suitable for officers and their families', to quote the local guidebook of the time.

Farnborough Court, 1909. This large house, built on land owned by St Michael's Abbey, was used as a Red Cross hospital for wounded Belgian soldiers during the First World War. Set in beautiful grounds, high on the hill to the left of Rectory Road, this was eventually demolished to make way for the building of the Abbey Way estate.

The Tumbledown Dick Hotel, *c.* 1920. Situated on Farnborough Road, and now overshadowed by the Kingsmead car-park, it is probably one of the earliest inns in Farnborough. There used to be a turnpike cottage nearby, the site of which is now buried beneath the Council offices car-park.

Farnborough Road at the junction with Oak Road, *c.* 1930. This quiet road used to wind peacefully up Star Hill, named after the Star Inn which stood just below, where Hillside was built. It is now a busy dual carriageway.

Farnborough & Cove War Memorial Cottage Hospital, *c.* 1921. A private house in Albert Road was converted into a twelve-bed hospital in memory of those who gave their lives in the First World War. It was opened by Earl Haig on 12 July 1921, but right from the outset money was needed for its upkeep and the local people were encouraged to support their new hospital. Many hospitals throughout the country required financial support, and on the right-hand gatepost is a poster advertising a competition run by Bovril, in which the first prize was £12,000 for a local hospital. Unfortunately Farnborough did not benefit from the competition; nevertheless the hospital expanded over the years and served the town well, until its services were taken over by Frimley Park Hospital. Today, as Devereux House, it is run as short stay accommodation and a day care centre. At that time, Albert Road was only a lane; it acted as the carriageway to Knellwood, whose white gates can be seen in the distance.

Reading Road, *c.* 1930. All the wide roads in this part of south Farnborough were designed in the 1860s by an architect, Mr Curry, who brought the idea from Eastbourne, another town he was engaged in developing. The houses here were built around the turn of the century and the one second from left, now demolished, was the home of Dr Hunter Dunn, one of the many doctors residing in the town.

Dr George Hunter Dunn, *c.* 1935. This well-loved man was a founder doctor of the cottage hospital and also gave his services to the wartime Red Cross hospital at Farnborough Court.

Miss Joan Hunter Dunn, 1934. The second daughter of Dr Hunter Dunn, her name has been immortalized in John Betjeman's 'The Subaltern's Love Song'. The poem was an imaginary story about someone he hardly knew. Apparently his descriptions of her life at that time were remarkably accurate, except that contrary to the last line of the poem he did not become 'engaged to Miss Joan Hunter Dunn'.

Farnborough Town Hall, Alexandra Road, *c.* 1903. This lovely building, symbolizing the growing prosperity of the town, was built in 1896 in the apex of Reading and Guildford Roads. Although made redundant by the new Council offices on Farnborough Road, it is now a listed building and has been refurbished as offices.

Alexandra Road at the crossroads with Reading and Guildford Roads, 1909. This was the view looking north, and the wideness of the roads is accentuated by the lack of traffic and housing. The town hall was to the left and St Mark's Church to the right.

Alpha Chambers, Alexandra Road, *c.* 1950. Occupied here by Dungay & Lee, the estate agents, this house had been built in the 1880s as one of an imposing row of large houses for use by serving officers. Fortunately most of the houses remain, though they are now in business use.

The southern end of Alexandra Road, *c.* 1902. The London & County Bank, now NatWest, is on the left and The Enterprise, next door, is receiving a delivery of coal.

The Conservative Club in Camp Road, *c.* 1910. This building was later purchased by T. Fenwick Harrison and presented to the YMCA as a memorial to servicemen who had given their lives for king and country.

The Avenue Electric Theatre, Camp Road, 1923. One of three cinemas in south Farnborough, it is now derelict. The others were the Scala across the road, now empty and the Empire Electric Theatre in Lynchford Road, now a motor cycle repair works.

The top end of Queen's Avenue, *c.* 1920. The omnibus advertising Thomas White & Co. is approaching Lynchford Road. All the houses have been pulled down, the road has been re-routed and the area has now been landscaped for amenity use.

The police houses on the corner of Winchester Street, *c.* 1910. Next door was the police station and behind were the stables. Peel Court now stands on the site.

The Queen's Hotel, *c*. 1900. This elegant structure, originally built of wood in about 1855 and later clad in bricks, formed an imposing landmark to welcome the traveller at the southernmost gateway of the town. In those days it commanded extensive views across the plains and gorse-covered heathlands. It had one hundred rooms and offered facilities such as pine therapeutic baths, the like of which could not be found in many places outside London. Frequently used by officers and dignitaries visiting the army at Aldershot, it numbered royalty among its patrons and also hosted many important civic dinners and functions of the day.

Catastrophe at the Queen's Hotel. On 14 May 1902 fire broke out in the basement and, because of its timber construction, quickly spread to engulf the whole hotel. At about a quarter to one, just as the guests were assembling for lunch, the alarm was raised and the whole hotel evacuated. Fortunately no one was hurt, although most of the guests and staff lost all their belongings. By one o'clock firemen from the Farnborough brigade, led by Capt. Fitch, were on the scene, soon to be joined by tenders from the Aldershot and Military brigades. The photograph was taken by Tudor Lawrence and shows military and civilian bystanders beside some of the furniture rescued from the building.

The next morning only the shell remained. This was the view which now greeted the visitor approaching along Lynchford Road. Yet another piece of tram track is visible, bottom right, this time from the days when trams ran to North Camp station.

The new Queen's Hotel, 1905. Two and a half years after the fire this Edwardian structure, so familiar today, had risen from the ashes to offer the most modern of hotel facilities, all lit by electricity and heated throughout by hot water radiators and pipes. In front, a hansom cab is still plying for trade alongside a newer mode of transport.

A sign of the times. By the outbreak of the First World War, facilities for the motor car were being offered, as shown by the sign pointing to the garage at the rear of the hotel. Today, despite its name change to the Forte Crest, the Queen's Hotel will always be the name etched on people's memories.

Cockadobby Hill, c. 1905. Through this book we have travelled from the old village, now called north Farnborough, to this southernmost point of the town. Thought to be the site of an old burial mound, it now forms part of the Queen's roundabout, on the road to Farnham. The simple inscription on the memorial reads: 'In memory of one who died for his country 1901'.

Acknowledgements

I would like to thank the residents of Farnborough and, in particular, the following individuals and organizations without whose assistance this book would not have been possible.

Aldershot Military Museum • A.J.A. Armstrong • J.W. Bartlett
Mrs I. Beavan • R.J. Cassidy • Mrs J. Chrismas • W. Croft • Mrs S.M. Darton
R.J. Debenham • Defence Research Agency © Crown Copyright, 1927 &
1911/DRA, Reproduced with the permission of the Controller, HMSO
DRA Farnborough Operatic Society • Revd C.G.H. Dunn • M.R. Evans
Farnborough Hill Convent • Farnborough Railway Enthusiasts Club
Mrs E. Fuller • R. Gibbens • A. Gosney • Mrs S. Grenham • Mrs I. Hamer
Farnborough Division Girl Guides • Hampshire County Library • Hampshire
Records Office, HRO56M71/470 Frith Collection • Hampshire Police
Historical Society • Dr P. Holmes • B.C. Kervell • Kingham's
B. Landymore • T.J. Lawrence • Dr and Mrs A. MacAdam • M. Maclay
R.D. McLaurin • V. Mitchell, co-author of *Woking to Southampton*
(Middleton Press) • W. Oakey • V. Richardson • Mrs I. Roberts • A. Rumble
R. Smith • L. Snowden • St Michael's Abbey • Miss B. Sheldon
Mrs C. Shepherd • Mrs M. Thomas • Mrs H. Tottle • Mr and Mrs P. Vickery
Mrs L. Walters • R. Yeoman.

Permission has been obtained to reproduce material and every effort has been made to establish copyright.

BRITAIN IN OLD PHOTOGRAPHS

To order any of these titles please telephone Littlehampton Book Services 01903 721596

ALDERNEY

Alderney: A Second Selection, *B Bonnard*

BEDFORDSHIRE

Bedfordshire at Work, *N Lutt*

BERKSHIRE

Maidenhead, *M Hayles & D Hedges*
Around Maidenhead, *M Hayles & B Hedges*
Reading, *P Southerton*
Reading: A Second Selection, *P Southerton*
Sandhurst and Crowthorne, *K Dancy*
Around Slough, *J Hunter & K Hunter*
Around Thatcham, *P Allen*
Around Windsor, *B Hedges*

BUCKINGHAMSHIRE

Buckingham and District, *R Cook*
High Wycombe, *R Goodearl*
Around Stony Stratford, *A Lambert*

CHESHIRE

Cheshire Railways, *M Hitches*
Chester, *S Nichols*

CLWYD

Clwyd Railways, *M Hitches*

CLYDESDALE

Clydesdale, *Lesmahagow Parish Historical Association*

CORNWALL

Cornish Coast, *T Bowden*
Falmouth, *P Gilson*
Lower Fal, *P Gilson*
Around Padstow, *M McCarthy*
Around Penzance, *J Holmes*
Penzance and Newlyn, *J Holmes*
Around Truro, *A Lyne*
Upper Fal, *P Gilson*

CUMBERLAND

Cockermouth and District, *J Bernard Bradbury*
Keswick and the Central Lakes, *J Marsh*
Around Penrith, *F Boyd*
Around Whitehaven, *H Fancy*

DERBYSHIRE

Derby, *D Buxton*
Around Matlock, *D Barton*

DEVON

Colyton and Seaton, *T Gosling*
Dawlish and Teignmouth, *G Gosling*
Devon Aerodromes, *K Saunders*
Exeter, *P Thomas*
Exmouth and Budleigh Salterton, *T Gosling*
From Haldon to Mid-Dartmoor, *T Hall*
Honiton and the Otter Valley, *J Yallop*
Around Kingsbridge, *K Tanner*
Around Seaton and Sidmouth, *T Gosling*
Seaton, Axminster and Lyme Regis, *T Gosling*

DORSET

Around Blandford Forum, *B Cox*
Bournemouth, *M Colman*
Bridport and the Bride Valley, *J Burrell & S Humphries*
Dorchester, *T Gosling*
Around Gillingham, *P Crocker*

DURHAM

Darlington, *G Flynn*
Darlington: A Second Selection, *G Flynn*
Durham People, *M Richardson*
Houghton-le-Spring and Hetton-le-Hole, *K Richardson*
Houghton-le-Spring and Hetton-le-Hole:
    A Second Selection, *K Richardson*
Sunderland, *S Miller & B Bell*
Teesdale, *D Coggins*
Teesdale: A Second Selection, *P Raine*
Weardale, *J Crosby*
Weardale: A Second Selection, *J Crosby*

DYFED

Aberystwyth and North Ceredigion,
    Dyfed Cultural Services Dept
Haverfordwest, *Dyfed Cultural Services Dept*
Upper Tywi Valley, *Dyfed Cultural Services Dept*

ESSEX

Around Grays, *B Evans*

GLOUCESTERSHIRE

Along the Avon from Stratford to Tewkesbury, *J Jeremiah*
Cheltenham: A Second Selection, *R Whiting*
Cheltenham at War, *P Gill*
Cirencester, *J Welsford*
Around Cirencester, *E Cuss & P Griffiths*
Forest, The, *D Mullin*
Gloucester, *J Voyce*
Around Gloucester, *A Sutton*
Gloucester: From the Walwin Collection, *J Voyce*
North Cotswolds, *D Viner*
Severn Vale, *A Sutton*
Stonehouse to Painswick, *A Sutton*
Stroud and the Five Valleys, *S Gardiner & L Padin*
Stroud and the Five Valleys: A Second Selection,
    S Gardiner & L Padin
Stroud's Golden Valley, *S Gardiner & L Padin*
Stroudwater and Thames & Severn Canals,
    E Cuss & S Gardiner
Stroudwater and Thames & Severn Canals: A Second
    Selection, *E Cuss & S Gardiner*
Tewkesbury and the Vale of Gloucester, *C Hilton*
Thornbury to Berkeley, *J Hudson*
Uley, Dursley and Cam, *A Sutton*
Wotton-under-Edge to Chipping Sodbury, *A Sutton*

GWYNEDD

Anglesey, *M Hitches*
Gwynedd Railways, *M Hitches*
Around Llandudno, *M Hitches*
Vale of Conwy, *M Hitches*

HAMPSHIRE

Gosport, *J Sadden*
Portsmouth, *P Rogers & D Francis*

HEREFORDSHIRE

Herefordshire, *A Sandford*

HERTFORDSHIRE

Barnet, *I Norrie*
Hitchin, *A Fleck*
St Albans, *S Mullins*
Stevenage, *M Appleton*

ISLE OF MAN

The Tourist Trophy, *B Snelling*

ISLE OF WIGHT

Newport, *D Parr*
Around Ryde, *D Parr*

JERSEY

Jersey: A Third Selection, *R Lemprière*

KENT

Bexley, *M Scott*
Broadstairs and St Peter's, *J Whyman*
Bromley, Keston and Hayes, *M Scott*
Canterbury: A Second Selection, *D Butler*
Chatham and Gillingham, *P MacDougall*
Chatham Dockyard, *P MacDougall*
Deal, *J Broady*
Early Broadstairs and St Peter's, *B Wootton*
East Kent at War, *D Collyer*
Eltham, *J Kennett*
Folkestone: A Second Selection, *A Taylor & E Rooney*
Goudhurst to Tenterden, *A Guilmant*
Gravesend, *R Hiscock*
Around Gravesham, *R Hiscock & D Grierson*
Herne Bay, *J Hawkins*
Lympne Airport, *D Collyer*
Maidstone, *I Hales*
Margate, *R Clements*
RAF Hawkinge, *R Humphreys*
RAF Manston, *RAF Manston History Club*
RAF Manston: A Second Selection,
    RAF Manston History Club
Ramsgate and Thanet Life, *D Perkins*
Romney Marsh, *E Carpenter*
Sandwich, *C Wanostrocht*
Around Tonbridge, *C Bell*
Tunbridge Wells, *M Rowlands & I Beavis*
Tunbridge Wells: A Second Selection,
    M Rowlands & I Beavis
Around Whitstable, *C Court*
Wingham, Adisham and Littlebourne, *M Crane*

LANCASHIRE

Around Barrow-in-Furness, *J Garbutt & J Marsh*
Blackpool, *C Rothwell*
Bury, *J Hudson*
Chorley and District, *J Smith*
Fleetwood, *C Rothwell*
Heywood, *J Hudson*
Around Kirkham, *C Rothwell*
Lancashire North of the Sands, *J Garbutt & J Marsh*
Around Lancaster, *S Ashworth*
Lytham St Anne's, *C Rothwell*
North Fylde, *C Rothwell*
Radcliffe, *J Hudson*
Rossendale, *B Moore & N Dunnachie*

LEICESTERSHIRE

Around Ashby-de-la-Zouch, *K Hillier*
Charnwood Forest, *I Keil, W Humphrey & D Wix*
Leicester, *D Burton*
Leicester: A Second Selection, *D Burton*
Melton Mowbray, *T Hickman*
Around Melton Mowbray, *T Hickman*
River Soar, *D Wix, P Shacklock & I Keil*
Rutland, *T Clough*
Vale of Belvoir, *T Hickman*
Around the Welland Valley, *S Mastoris*

LINCOLNSHIRE

Grimsby, *J Tierney*
Around Grimsby, *J Tierney*
Grimsby Docks, *J Tierney*
Lincoln, *D Cuppleditch*

Scunthorpe, *D Taylor*
Skegness, *W Kime*
Around Skegness, *W Kime*

LONDON

Balham and Tooting, *P Loobey*
Crystal Palace, Penge & Anerley, *M Scott*
Greenwich and Woolwich, *K Clark*
Hackney: A Second Selection, *D Mander*
Lewisham and Deptford, *J Coulter*
Lewisham and Deptford: A Second Selection, *J Coulter*
Streatham, *P Loobey*
Around Whetstone and North Finchley, *J Heathfield*
Woolwich, *B Evans*

MONMOUTHSHIRE

Chepstow and the River Wye, *A Rainsbury*
Monmouth and the River Wye, *Monmouth Museum*

NORFOLK

Great Yarmouth, *M Teun*
Norwich, *M Colman*
Wymondham and Attleborough, *P Yaxley*

NORTHAMPTONSHIRE

Around Stony Stratford, *A Lambert*

NOTTINGHAMSHIRE

Arnold and Bestwood, *M Spick*
Arnold and Bestwood: A Second Selection, *M Spick*
Changing Face of Nottingham, *G Oldfield*
Mansfield, *Old Mansfield Society*
Around Newark, *T Warner*
Nottingham: 1944–1974, *D Whitworth*
Sherwood Forest, *D Ottewell*
Victorian Nottingham, *M Payne*

OXFORDSHIRE

Around Abingdon, *P Horn*
Banburyshire, *M Barnett & S Gosling*
Burford, *A Jewell*
Around Didcot and the Hagbournes, *B Lingham*
Garsington, *M Gunther*
Around Henley-on-Thames, *S Ellis*
Oxford: The University, *J Rhodes*
Thame to Watlington, *N Hood*
Around Wallingford, *D Beasley*
Witney, *T Worley*
Around Witney, *C Mitchell*
Witney District, *T Worley*
Around Woodstock, *J Bond*

POWYS

Brecon, *Brecknock Museum*
Welshpool, *E Bredsdorff*

SHROPSHIRE

Shrewsbury, *D Trumper*
Whitchurch to Market Drayton, *M Morris*

SOMERSET

Bath, *J Hudson*
Bridgwater and the River Parrett, *R Fitzhugh*
Bristol, *D Moorcroft & N Campbell-Sharp*
Changing Face of Keynsham,
   B Lowe & M Whitehead

Chard and Ilminster, *G Gosling & F Huddy*
Crewkerne and the Ham Stone Villages,
   G Gosling & F Huddy
Around Keynsham and Saltford, *B Lowe & T Brown*
Midsomer Norton and Radstock, *C Howell*
Somerton, Ilchester and Langport, *G Gosling & F Huddy*
Taunton, *N Chipchase*
Around Taunton, *N Chipchase*
Wells, *C Howell*
Weston-Super-Mare, *S Poole*
Around Weston-Super-Mare, *S Poole*
West Somerset Villages, *K Houghton & L Thomas*

STAFFORDSHIRE

Aldridge, *J Farrow*
Bilston, *E Rees*
Black Country Transport: Aviation, *A Brew*
Around Burton upon Trent, *G Sowerby & R Farman*
Bushbury, *A Chatwin, M Mills & E Rees*
Around Cannock, *M Mills & S Belcher*
Around Leek, *R Poole*
Lichfield, *H Clayton & K Simmons*
Around Pattingham and Wombourne, *M Griffiths,*
   P Leigh & M Mills
Around Rugeley, *T Randall & J Anslow*
Smethwick, *J Maddison*
Stafford, *J Anslow & T Randall*
Around Stafford, *J Anslow & T Randall*
Stoke-on-Trent, *I Lawley*
Around Tamworth, *R Sulima*
Around Tettenhall and Codsall, *M Mills*
Tipton, Wednesbury and Darlaston, *R Pearson*
Walsall, *D Gilbert & M Lewis*
Wednesbury, *I Bott*
West Bromwich, *R Pearson*

SUFFOLK

Ipswich: A Second Selection, *D Kindred*
Around Ipswich, *D Kindred*
Around Mildenhall, *C Dring*
Southwold to Aldeburgh, *H Phelps*
Around Woodbridge, *H Phelps*

SURREY

Cheam and Belmont, *P Berry*
Croydon, *S Bligh*
Dorking and District, *K Harding*
Around Dorking, *A Jackson*
Around Epsom, *P Berry*
Farnham: A Second Selection, *J Parratt*
Around Haslemere and Hindhead, *T Winter & G Collyer*
Richmond, *Richmond Local History Society*
Sutton, *P Berry*

SUSSEX

Arundel and the Arun Valley, *J Godfrey*
Bishopstone and Seaford, *P Pople & P Berry*
Brighton and Hove, *J Middleton*
Brighton and Hove: A Second Selection, *J Middleton*
Around Crawley, *M Goldsmith*
Hastings, *P Haines*
Hastings: A Second Selection, *P Haines*
Around Haywards Heath, *J Middleton*
Around Heathfield, *A Gillet & B Russell*
Around Heathfield: A Second Selection,
   A Gillet & B Russell
High Weald, *B Harwood*
High Weald: A Second Selection, *B Harwood*
Horsham and District, *T Wales*

Lewes, *J Middleton*
RAF Tangmere, *A Saunders*
Around Rye, *A Dickinson*
Around Worthing, *S White*

WARWICKSHIRE

Along the Avon from Stratford to Tewkesbury, *J Jeremiah*
Bedworth, *J Burton*
Coventry, *D McGrory*
Around Coventry, *D McGrory*
Nuneaton, *S Clews & S Vaughan*
Around Royal Leamington Spa, *J Cameron*
Around Royal Leamington Spa: A Second Selection,
   J Cameron
Around Warwick, *R Booth*

WESTMORLAND

Eden Valley, *J Marsh*
Kendal, *M & P Duff*
South Westmorland Villages, *J Marsh*
Westmorland Lakes, *J Marsh*

WILTSHIRE

Around Amesbury, *P Daniels*
Chippenham and Lacock, *A Wilson & M Wilson*
Around Corsham and Box, *A Wilson & M Wilson*
Around Devizes, *D Buxton*
Around Highworth, *G Tanner*
Around Highworth and Faringdon, *G Tanner*
Around Malmesbury, *A Wilson*
Marlborough: A Second Selection, *P Colman*
Around Melksham,
   Melksham and District Historical Association
Nadder Valley, *R. Sawyer*
Salisbury, *P Saunders*
Salisbury: A Second Selection, *P Daniels*
Salisbury: A Third Selection, *P Daniels*
Around Salisbury, *P Daniels*
Swindon: A Third Selection, *The Swindon Society*
Swindon: A Fourth Selection, *The Swindon Society*
Trowbridge, *M Marshman*
Around Wilton, *P Daniels*
Around Wootton Bassett, Cricklade and Purton, *T Sharp*

WORCESTERSHIRE

Evesham to Bredon, *F Archer*
Around Malvern, *K Smith*
Around Pershore, *M Dowty*
Redditch and the Needle District, *R Saunders*
Redditch: A Second Selection, *R Saunders*
Around Tenbury Wells, *D Green*
Worcester, *M Dowty*
Around Worcester, *R Jones*
Worcester in a Day, *M Dowty*
Worcestershire at Work, *R Jones*

YORKSHIRE

Huddersfield: A Second Selection, *H Wheeler*
Huddersfield: A Third Selection, *H Wheeler*
Leeds Road and Rail, *R Vickers*
Pontefract, *R van Riel*
Scarborough, *D Coggins*
Scarborough's War Years, *R Percy*
Skipton and the Dales, *Friends of the Craven Museum*
Around Skipton-in-Craven, *Friends of the Craven Museum*
Yorkshire Wolds, *I & M Sumner*